Whale Sharks

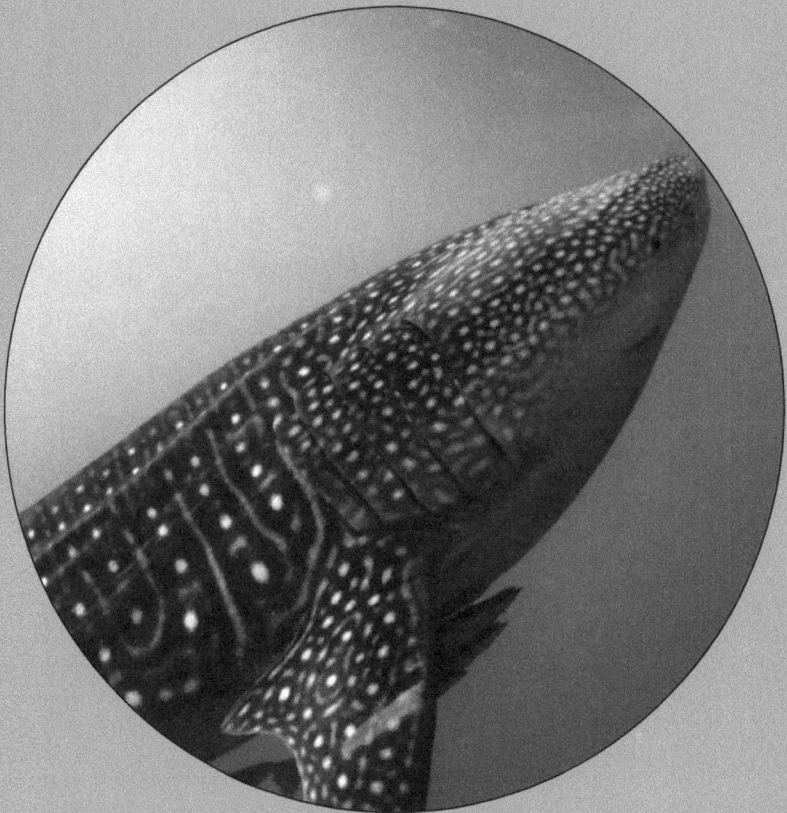

Victoria Blakemore

For Mom, with love

Copyright info/picture credits

Table of Contents

What Are Whale Sharks?

Whale sharks are the largest shark. They are also the largest fish. Whale sharks are related to other sharks such as nurse sharks and bamboo sharks.

Whale sharks get their name from their large size. They are closer in size to whales than to other sharks.

Whale sharks are a mixture of gray, tan, and white. They have spots and stripes on their back and head.

3

Size

Most whale sharks grow to be between twenty and twenty-five feet long. Some grow to be over forty feet long.

Whale sharks can **vary** in weight. Some can grow to weigh over 40,000 pounds.

Female whale sharks are

usually larger than male

whale sharks.

Physical Characteristics

Whale sharks have large gills on the side of their body.

Their gills filter out oxygen from the water so they can breathe.

They have a long, strong tail that is used to **propel** them forward in the water.

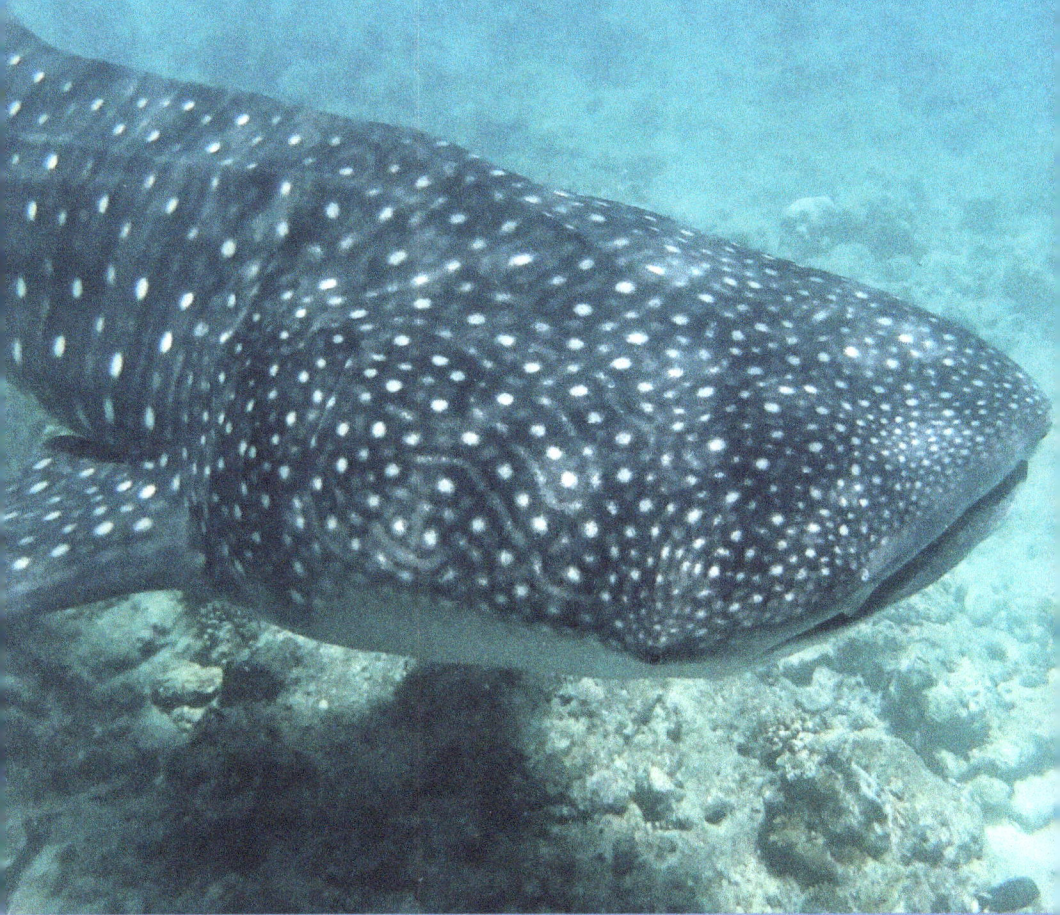

Whale sharks have a special pattern of spots and stripes. Their pattern is like a human fingerprint, no two whale sharks are exactly the same.

Habitat

Whale sharks are found in warm, tropical waters. They are usually found in waters around the **equator**.

In the spring, whale sharks **migrate** to the waters around Australia. Researchers believe this is because of the amount of plankton found there.

Range

Whale sharks are found around North America, Africa, Asia, South America, and Australia.

They are not found around Antarctica or Europe. The waters there are too cold for them.

Diet

Whale sharks are **omnivores**.

They eat meat and plants.

They usually eat plankton,

which is made up of tiny

plants and animals. They

have also been known to eat

small fish, squids, and plants.

Whale shark eyes are on the sides of their head. Researchers believe they use their sense of smell to find food.

Whale sharks are one of three kinds of sharks that are filter-feeders. They do not hunt fish like most other sharks.

They open their large mouth and suck in a mouthful of water. The water is strained out through their gills. This leaves the plankton for them to eat.

Whale sharks have thousands of

tiny teeth, but they do not need

them to eat plankton.

Communication

Not much is known about how whale sharks communicate with each other. They aren't seen together often and it can be hard to study them.

It is thought that they communicate like other sharks, through movement and sensing vibrations in the water.

Like other sharks, whale

sharks cannot make sounds.

Movement

Whale sharks move slowly in the water. They often swim at about three miles per hour.

They have large **pectoral fins** and **dorsal fins**. Their fins help them to steer and remain **stable** in the water. Their powerful tail is what makes them move.

Whale sharks spend a lot of their time swimming slowly with their mouth open to feed.

Whale Shark Pups

Whale sharks can have about 300 babies. Their babies are called pups. The pups hatch from their eggs inside the mother, then are born.

Although whale sharks have a lot of pups, many don't survive to adulthood because of predators.

Whale sharks are able to start

having pups by the time they

are about twenty-five years old.

Whale Shark Life

Whale sharks are usually **solitary**. They spend most of their time alone. They are sometimes seen in groups when they are feeding.

They are known to travel long distances. One whale shark traveled over 12,000 miles in less than three years.

Whale sharks often dive very
deep. They are sometimes seen
close to the surface.

Diving with Whale Sharks

Whale sharks are very gentle creatures. They are very unlikely to attack humans. Some people like to dive with whale sharks.

Some people travel to places where whale sharks are found just to get a chance to dive with them.

There is no record of a whale shark attacking a human. A whale shark's tail could injure a diver if the diver got too close.

Population

Whale sharks are **endangered**. There are not many left in the wild. They could become **extinct** if their population continues to **decline**.

Researchers are not sure exactly how many whale sharks are left. They are very hard to find and count **accurately**.

No one is sure exactly how long whale sharks can live. It is thought that they can live over seventy years.

Whale Sharks in Danger

Whale sharks are facing several threats, all of which are because of humans. The main threat to whale sharks is that they are caught for their oil, fins, skin, and meat.

Whale sharks can also be hit by boats or caught by fishermen by mistake.

Whale sharks can become

tangled up in nets used to

catch fish.

Helping Whale Sharks

Many countries have laws against catching whale sharks. These laws are one way people are trying to help whale sharks.

Certain fishing nets that are known to catch whale sharks have been **banned** in areas where they are found.

Some habitats where whale sharks are known to be are now protected habitats. Fishing of any kind is not allowed there.

Researchers are studying whale sharks. They hope that learning more about them will allow us to help them more.

Glossary

Accurately: free of mistakes, correct

Banned: forbidden, having a law against

Decline: to decrease, get smaller

Dorsal fins: the fins on the top of animals

Endangered: at risk of becoming extinct

Equator: the imaginary line that goes around the middle of the earth

Extinct: when there are no more of an animal left in the wild

Migrate: to travel from one place to another

Omnivore: an animal that eats meat and plants

Pectoral fins: the fins on the side of an animal

Propel: to push forward

Solitary: living alone

Stable: steady in position

Vary: differ

About the Author

Victoria Blakemore is a first grade

teacher in Southwest Florida with a

passion for reading.

You can visit her at

www.elementaryexplorers.com

Also in This Series

Gray Wolves	Sloths	Flamingos	Camels	Koalas	Honey Bees	Pandas
Pangolins	White-Tailed Deer	Orcas	Giraffes	Corn	Meerkats	Echidnas
Walruses	Raccoons	Bald Eagles	Apples	Arctic Foxes	Red Pandas	Cassowaries
Tigers	Ladybugs	Moose	Beluga Whales	Leopards	Elephants	Jellyfish
Binturongs	Lions	Dolphins	Reindeer	Hammerhead Sharks	Hippos	Pumpkins
Peafowl	Chameleons	Florida Panthers	Aye-Ayes	Black Bears	Cheetahs	Manatees
Gingerbread	Polar Bears	Hot Chocolate	Orangutans	Coyotes	Marshmallows	Strawberries

Victoria Blakemore

Also in This Series

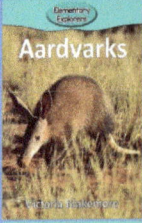

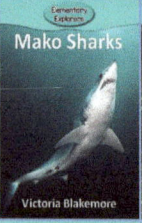

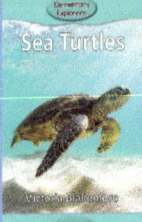

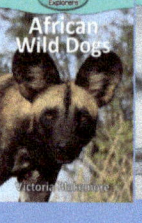

Aardvarks	Mako Sharks	Alligators	Frogs	Hedgehogs	Brown Bears	Bongos
Sea Turtles	Quokkas	Muskrats	Zebras	Red Foxes	Ring-Tailed Lemurs	Platypuses
Anteaters	Kangaroos	Rhinos	Jaguars	Wombats	Capybaras	Gorillas
Cats	Skunks	Butterflies	Dingoes	Snow Leopards	African Wild Dogs	Penguins
Whale Sharks	Wolverines	Warthogs	Caracals			

Victoria Blakemore

www.ingramcontent.com/pod-product-compliance
Lightning Source LLC
Chambersburg PA
CBHW051254020426
42333CB00025B/3208